SECRETS OF FRANCHISE SUCCESS

The Formula for Becoming and Staying a Top Producing Franchisee

Marc Camras, PhD & Melissa Hart Woods

INDIE BOOKS
INTERNATIONAL

ISBN: 1-941870-10-4
ISBN 13: 978-1-941870-10-5
Library of Congress Control Number: 2014958999

Designed by Joni McPherson, mcphersongraphics.com

INDIE BOOKS INTERNATIONAL, LLC
2424 VISTA WAY, SUITE 316
OCEANSIDE, CA 92054

www.indiebooksintl.com

CONTENTS

✳

ACKNOWLEDGEMENTS

This book began almost five years ago after numerous discussions we had with Mitch Simon about bringing coaching and leadership practices into the world of franchising. We would like to thank Mitch for his support, energy, and office space as we collected and analyzed data, and developed an outline for the book. The book would also not be written if it weren't for the franchisors who provided access to their franchisees, and those franchisees who generously took time out from running their businesses to talk with us about what made them successful. In appreciation of their time and insights we want to thank the following franchisees:

Alan Cohen, Tutoring Club
Anil Nanda, Expense Reduction Analysts
Anne Krajewski, Renue Systems
Ben Knight, FASTSIGNS
Bill Holden, LaVida Massage
Bill Syvertsen, Tutoring Club
Bob Borkovec, Furniture Medic
Bob White, The Maids
Brad Little, Case Design
Brad Whitt, Sport Clips
Cheri McEssy, BrightStar

Chris Ashcraft, Express Employment Professionals

Connie Worrel, Express Employment Professionals

Dan Austad, Good Feet

Dana Raley, Sport Clips

Dave and Linda Skromme, FASTSIGNS

Dean Bingham, Mr. Transmission

Donna Ojjeh, The Maids

Eric Kaplan, Good Feet

Greg Massa, BrightStar

Gwen Heim, La Vida Massage

Jason Klassen, Furniture Medic

Jay Pond, Mr. Transmission

Jeff Boehmer, Aussie Pet Mobile

Jeff Harig, FASTSIGNS

Jim Duncan, AIM Mail Centers

Jim Kabel, CASE Design

Jimmy Mitchell, Mr. Transmission

John Botsko, BrightStar

Leon Feuerberg, Aussie Pet Mobile

Mary Bigler, Maui Wowi Hawaiian

Michele Ganela, Gotcha Covered

Miguel Portillo, Wings Pizza N Things

Mike Lee, AIM Mail Centers

Mike Mack, ServiceMaster Clean

Nick Bradshaw, Service Team Of Professionals

Ric and Kathy Ferwerda, 1-800 DryClean

Rich Emery, ServiceMaster Clean

Rick Garman, The Maids

Rob Formanek, Friendly Computers
Rocky Gill, Express Employment Professionals
Ryan Cook, SNAP Fitness
Scott Bradish, Sport Clips
Scott Schumacher, Service Team of Professionals
Scott Suryan, Maui Wowi Hawaiian
Shane Ortel, Gotcha Covered
Shawn Folks, Service Team of Professionals
Tara Belzer, Friendly Mobile Computers
Will Lawrence, Play N Trade

PREFACE

*

THE FRANCHISEE FORMULA

Marketing x Metrics x Resources x Leadership x Mindset =
FRANCHISEE SUCCESS

FIRST
THINGS
FIRST

CHAPTER 1

✳

The Formula for Growing Your Franchise

"I wanted to control my own destiny. Disliked corporate America. I hated being treated like a number. Wanted to live in the area where I wanted to live. Tired of traveling and not home for dinner. I never had the full ability to make my own decisions. I always had to report to someone. I felt stifled. I would rather work hard for me and the benefit of the community, not for the benefit of the stockholders."

JOHN BOTSKO, BRIGHTSTAR CARE FRANCHISEE

H ere is the good news for franchisees. The dream of being a top 20 percent franchisee in any system is alive and doing well, if you take the time to learn how others have done it and then apply that knowledge. This book contains the secrets of franchisees who perform in the top 20 percent of their systems. Secrets are drawn from the proprietary research conducted with business owners from a variety of franchise systems.

The majority of people who purchase a franchise business (we will call them "frantreprenuers") do it hoping to replace the sense of imprisonment that comes from a nine-to-five job where they make money for someone else and follow someone else's rules. They have a strong belief that owning their own business with a system and a proven track record will give them more control over their time, schedule, earning potential, and future. Unfortunately, many of these folks also believe that buying a franchise is like buying an extra pair of hands that will do most of the heavy lifting. Very often, these franchisees are disappointed. They work longer hours, and earn less than they did as an employee. Some dream of going back to that nine-to-five job and collecting a paycheck.

This book is focused 1) on those franchisees who have not achieved the success they wanted, 2) those who are thinking about becoming franchise business owners, and 3) anyone else who has ever wondered what it takes to be a top 20 percent business owner. Because we are your researchers and guides, allow us to introduce ourselves. As franchise experts and business coaches, we have been working successfully with new franchisees and business owners for close to two decades, so we are well-versed regarding their successes and frustrations. Marc Camras has a PhD in Human Information Processing, has coached executives and entrepreneurs for a decade, and prior to that was a partner in a highly recommended HR consulting business. For the past nine years, he has worked successfully with wannabe entrepreneurs and frantrepreneurs, connecting them with franchise companies that are a match for their interests, skills, and goals, and prepared them for business ownership. Melissa Woods started a brick-and-mortar kids gym, franchised it (internationally), and sold it. After the sale of her company she went to work as the Director of Coaching at OneCoach, an international business coaching company. Now she coaches and consults with business owners across a range of industries interested in increasing their profits and gaining market exposure.

As friends and colleagues with our own separate consulting/coaching businesses, we began a ritual of weekly lunch meetings to share new practices and ideas for business owners. Marc's original idea was to connect the world of coaching to the franchise world through a book that would capture the obstacles and opportunities faced by franchisees. Based on her years of running her own franchise company and attending multiple International Franchise Association conventions, Melissa was astounded at how all franchise systems, whether big (over 200 franchisees) or small (under twenty-five franchisees) struggled with the same issues. In our conversations with several hundred franchisors over the past two decades, we found plenty of anecdotal evidence of an 80/20 rule that exists within all franchise systems. Twenty percent of franchisees are very successful, while eighty percent of franchisees are moderately successful, slightly successful, or struggling. While we did not find anything in the literature on franchise business success that pertained to the 80/20 rule, we heard over and over again that regardless of whether a franchise sold a product or a service, whether it was a new franchise or an old one, whether it had a few thousand units, or less than fifty units, the 80/20 rule still applied. Over a two-year period, we interviewed over fifty franchisees from twenty five different franchise companies in a broad mix of industries whose franchisors considered them to be in their top 20 percent. When we spoke with franchisors about having their franchisees participate in our research, we were clear that we did not want their number one or number two producers. We recognized that being number one or number two in anything can be extremely difficult, and believed our readers would be more likely to connect with the plain vanilla top 20 percent producers.

We wanted to know more about how these top 20 percent franchisees maintained their positions in the top tier of their respective franchise systems over time. We were curious if there was a common thread that ran among these top 20 percent producers or if there was a unique set of circumstances that distinguished them from others in their systems. Rather than rely on our own experiences to tell a story, we wanted those with boots on the ground to share their stories. We were interested in 1) What these owners could tell us about taking a business model and a system and making it an extraordinary business, 2) Why these owners were able to find greater success than their peers, and 3) What our interview data would reveal about small-business owners in general. We spent the next year putting the interview data into categories. As we analyzed the data from all the frantrepreneurs we interviewed, we were able to identify common traits and practices shared by most of these franchisees. We call these common traits and practices "The Secret Formula," and use the interview data to help the reader understand what is needed to achieve greater success.

Our mission is to share what we learned in our interviews and demonstrate these traits and practices through a series of action steps at the end of each section that could be applied by current and future business owners in their own journey from mediocrity to success. We also want to stress that while this book is about franchisees, most of the information revealed is applicable to any small-business owner. We are not only including *what* our franchisees bring to the table and what they do—we are also including *how* they do it.

During our interviews with the franchisees, we met many

frantrepreneurs who were fed up with corporate America and its vapid promises. We met business owners such as Mary Bigler, who worked for years in a family roofing business before becoming a stay-at-home mom and then a Maui Wowi franchisee; and Rocky Gill, who was an accountant and later spent over a decade working as a controller for a large health care company before becoming an Express Employment Professionals franchisee. All our interviewees were committed to being in charge of their own destinies. We found people who were fascinated with who they could become, committed to taking 100 percent responsibility for what they truly cared about, and passionate about the change they went through while facing obstacles along the way.

We recognize that *quality* franchisors provide their incoming franchisees with an operations manual and training so that new franchisees can spend their first year learning about the business and how to run it. After the first year, many of these franchisees get so comfortable in operations mode that they either don't know what else to do, or are afraid to step out and explore what it takes to be a top producer. This is the exact point when they need to start spending more time thinking about what it takes to be a top 20 percent business owner. We intend to give hope to an audience that wants to know how to take their financial future into their own hands despite the uncertainty that business ownership creates. To be the best requires a growth mindset, an orientation around making contributions to others, and the openness to change which many say they have, but do not possess.

The book is comprised of five sections. The first four sections are comprised of what we call "The Outside Game." This includes daily operations that take into account systems and processes, management, leadership, marketing, metrics, and finance. The last section is what we call "The Inside Game." This consists of how one thinks about business, and reflects the importance of our inner dialogue, attitudes, and mindset. By sharing information collected from some of the franchisee heroes and heroines who make up this great nation, we hope to reignite your entrepreneurial spirit and inspire you to greater success. You may be more committed to achieving greater success in your business, or have a renewed sense of purpose and direction in your second, third, or fourth business. You may have just needed a few nudges and some direction in how to better market your business or manage your employees, and this book will provide you with that. You may even be inspired to make the break you have been waiting for and become a business/franchise owner. Others will put the book down and finally be able to say, "Owning my own business is not a good idea." We hope you find what you need in this book to start you on a path to improving your future.

It has been estimated that there are well over 300 industries that use franchising to distribute goods and services to consumers—and close to 3000 franchise companies that exist in any given year. It is estimated that a new franchise opens every eight minutes. Recent estimates from the International Franchise Association suggest that one in twelve businesses in the United States is a franchise. According to its research and Census Bureau data from 2010, there are expected to be about 770,000 franchise businesses by the end of 2014, which will employ somewhere around 8.5 million people (out of 59 million employees in the United States), and have estimated revenues of somewhere between $839 billion to $1.3 trillion. Business format franchises continue to have a profound effect on our economy as more and more people leave the workforce and re-emerge as business owners.

Our research can be summed up in The Franchisee Formula that contains five variables:

Marketing x Metrics x Resources x Leadership x Mindset =
FRANCHISEE SUCCESS

We believe that adding time and effort to one variable will have a multiplier effect on a business owner's success.

SECTION ONE:
MARKETING

CHAPTER 2

*

Master the Marketing

"Following the marketing system the franchisor gave me helped in my success, but it wasn't 'the magic bullet.' For anyone looking to buy a franchise, there are two things critically important. You must be confident and understand the business model you are selling."

BOB WHITE, THE MAIDS FRANCHISEE

M arketing is an essential component to every business strategy. It is the process of communicating the value of a product or service to customers, for the purpose of influencing customers' behavior and buying decisions. Buying a franchise provides a new business owner with a guide for building brand awareness. During their initial training, a new franchisee receives an Operations Manual that includes a proprietary system for marketing. They also receive marketing material in the form of brochures, websites, mailers, and details as to when and how to distribute the material and respond to customers. Franchisors can provide guidance as to how to tap into your market in a big, small, or medium-size city, how to get more customers, get repeat customers, and find new ways to provide service to their customers.

But, they can't tell you what is particularly unique about your own community, and how best to integrate yourself into it. What we found in our research is that top 20 percent producers are involved in their communities in multiple ways, and believe that their involvement is integral to building good will for their business. Building good will creates loyalty and helps franchisees develop relationships with their customers by attaching their brand to the causes and the people in their community. In this section we will demonstrate the four aspects of marketing that the top 20 percent producers focused on.

CHAPTER 3

*

Understand the Customer

"People want to be treated special. Delivering a superior customer experience is one of the most important marketing strategies you can have. Ultimately, it's about building relationships and making every customer feel special and important."

JOHN BOTSKO, BRIGHTSTAR CARE FRANCHISEE

Most of our interviewees not only paid close attention to their customers' purchasing behaviors, they also found opportunities to talk to them. They viewed their marketing plans as dynamic rather than static. Based on the information they mined from customers, their marketing actions were continually evolving and changing. They paid attention to what was working and not working and used their marketing plan to guide their decisions and actions. Through conversations with customers, they were able to find new ways of delighting them. These conversations allowed them to continually add, test, and improve their services/products through the information they gleaned. Listening to their customers, coupled with an understanding of what their competition was or was not doing, provided franchisees with important information that could improve upon the customer's experience.

We call this an "in the trenches" mentality. The best way to do this was to have direct contact with customers. This meant being in the store on the floor if it was a business-to-consumer model. If it was a business-to-business model, picking up the phone, or better yet, driving to see their clients on a regular basis was an important part of their marketing strategy. From a place of curiosity, their approach was to find out the truth about how their customers interacted with the brand and what their overall experiences were. By opening up conversations and asking questions such as: How's everything going—

> *
>
> **Listening to their customers, coupled with an understanding of what their competition was or was not doing, provided franchisees with important information that could improve upon the customer's experience.**
>
> *

are you happy with our service? How could we be making you happier? What do you wish we provided that we don't? They were able to dig deeper to find out who their customers were, what their pain points were, and how their brand could help solve their problems and make their life a little better.

The information from these conversations helped the franchise owners know what they were doing well, what was missing, and best of all, how to improve. The prevailing philosophy of all of the top 20 percent was that customer feedback was essential to pleasing the customer and keeping them happy, connected to the brand, loyal, and most importantly, singing their praises to everyone they knew. One franchisee we spoke with who owned a restaurant model said it perfectly, "Let your customer be your University."

CHAPTER 4

*

Deliver Mind-Blowing Customer Service

Whether the franchise is a business-to-consumer model or a business-to-business model, without a group of loyal customers plus a steady flow of new customers, the business cannot be successful. The acquisition of new customers requires spending marketing dollars, and that amount is often significantly more than what a franchisor requires. An equally important marketing technique and cost-effective approach is providing an outstanding experience for the customer. By listening to the customer, the franchisees we interviewed were also building trusting relationships. Staying engaged with customers regularly insured they had a pulse on what was working and what wasn't working and what their customers wished they did more of. Trusting relationships translated to raving fans (i.e., brand ambassadors who acted as referral partners). These top 20 producers did not underestimate the power of word of mouth. Instead, they saw it as another important marketing approach.

When we asked the franchisees, "How do you stand out in the market and keep customers, and how do you continually sell more services to your existing customers?" this is what we heard:

1. Know who your competition is, and what they do and don't do well.
2. Take time to listen to your customer.
3. Take the feedback you get from customers and implement new ways to tweak operations to continually provide a better experience.
4. Track how new concepts are received and how they can be improved upon.
5. Get rid of strategies that are not working. As one of our franchisees said, "If every decision we make from the top down has the customer experience in mind, we will continually be growing."

By focusing on what differentiated them from their competition, our franchisees stood out. They studied the gaps in how their competition provided goods and services and then demonstrated how they were different. Many of these tactics were simple little tweaks that told the customer, "You are important to us. We care about you and want to make you feel special." Several of the franchisees used formal surveys and rewarded their customers with free products or services to complete them. Others persuaded customers to like them on Facebook in return for a gift or coupon of some kind. Angie's List and Yelp were also brand enhancers used by many of the franchises we interviewed who had service model businesses. Most of the franchisees we interviewed understood the importance of staying current with the social media venues that allowed them to best communicate their brand. Here are some real examples of what the top 20 percent producers did to improve upon and constantly delight their customers.

One of our interviewees ran a handyman and remodeling business. For this business owner, professionalism was a huge differentiator from his competitors. He focused on things like showing up on time, having clean and neat uniforms, and calling before they came. Doing research about the competitors in the same space revealed that many of them were missing this approach. His company also backed up all their work with a one-year warranty, and because it was a service business not just a project business, they emphasized to the customer the process in place to minimize disruptions to a family.

> *
>
> **By focusing on what differentiated them from their competition, our franchisees stood out.**
>
> *

Another franchisee we interviewed owned a haircut business. He was willing to do whatever it took to satisfy his customers, and shared that he went further than any other franchise owner in his system to make his customers happy. For instance, when it was brought to his attention that one of his clients was not happy with a haircut, he chased him down outside the store and offered him free haircuts for the year. Not only did he earn back his trust, this customer was so thrilled that he shared the experience with others, which resulted in more customers for the salon owner.

The owner of a massage franchise instituted a pre- and post-visit evaluation to gauge his customer's experiences. He felt it was important to know what their expectations were ahead of time so the massage therapists understood exactly what they needed and could deliver it to them. A fitness franchise owner mentioned that his differentiator was to go above and beyond what the competition was doing. He always had extremely clean gyms and extra touches like fresh flowers in the reception and the bathrooms.

A last example comes from a commercial cleaning franchisee. He developed a program for his employees called Master Moments. Employees were rewarded for finding efficient and profitable ways to create above and beyond moments for the customer. The program was a success and he collected over 200 Master Moments from his employees and shared them with his customers.

CHAPTER 5

*

Commit to Community Involvement

"I am a visible icon in my community from every perspective. I show up. Serve – I enjoy it."

JIM DUNCAN, AIM MAIL CENTERS FRANCHISEE

W e learned from our franchisees that a key to getting your business working well is learning how to create a marketing plan that shows the community that you understand what their needs are and that you care about them. One franchisee shared that every marketing action you take must be about how you will serve your community. Some of our franchisees built goodwill for their business by becoming fundraisers for local community organizations. Business owners willing to head up fundraising efforts created a buzz and a loyal following. Their efforts not only help the community, they also link the name of the franchisee's business to a cause that serves the community. The franchisee's brand becomes synonymous with the community/organization they support.

One franchise owner we interviewed was involved in Operation Uplink – an organization that raises money for soldiers to call home on the holidays. Another established a scholarship program in a couple of high schools that recognized kids who had jobs and high GPAs. In that program ten students received $500 awards each year from this franchisee, and other businesses in the community were brought in by the franchisee to help support the award luncheons. Another franchisee worked Grad Nights as the top security person, and gave money to a number of school's Booster Clubs. These franchisees became visible icons in their community that people knew and appreciated. These successful franchisees were thinking less about how the community would support their business, and more about how they could better serve their community so that the community had a brighter future. Orienting around serving their community led to more business.

CHAPTER 6
Network without "Networking"

"You have to be willing to talk to people, face to face, eyeball to eyeball."

DANA RALEY, SPORT CLIPS FRANCHISEE

"Can't be afraid of rejection. Must have that built in ability to talk to people. You can hire people to run your business but you must be the billboard."

BILL SYVERTSEN, TUTORING CLUB FRANCHISEE

Another common trait shared by our top 20 percent producers was that they did not hide behind operations. They made a point to get away from their businesses, meet other people in the community, and develop relationships. Some of them called it networking, but most of them referred to this practice as building relationships. Many of them joined formal business networking groups or trade groups. Many interviewees shared that anytime they stepped out of their actual business they were in "networking mode." Whether going to the market, the dry cleaners, picking up their kids at school, or going to a social function, the owners talked to people about their business.

Their interactions in the community were not necessarily from a sales perspective, they were instead an opportunity to educate people about the benefits of a service or product. They made a point of having conversations that appealed to each person they were talking to by asking what that person's needs were.

Finding creative ways to build relationships with partners was another tactic of networking. One of our smoothie and coffee franchisees researched who the top event planners were in her community. On the hottest days of the year she brought in free smoothies to everyone in their offices. "We were shocked at how many connections we made simply because we gave them a treat when they needed it. It translated directly into more business."

Business-to-business networking is all about building relationships. Our interviewees shared that relationship building has to do with sharing your passion about the product or service you provide. Unlike a business-to-consumer marketing plan, a business-to-business plan does not have the same variety of options for acquiring new clients, such as billboards, print, TV ads, and social media. Therefore, building relationships is a key to succeeding in the B-to-B market. One franchisee shared his "Johnny Appleseed" theory—he plants lots of seeds and eventually, they start to grow into real business. A commercial cleaning franchisee we interviewed admitted that when he first opened his business, rejection was not easy. In the early days, he had a major competitor who grew up in the market while he came from out of state. His competitor had most of the major buildings tied up. He'd take care of building engineers with perks, and was friends with the building owners. The quality of service didn't matter because he had relationships and took care of everyone involved in the buildings. In response, our interviewee got more involved in corporate events and functions. He continued to make sales calls. Eventually, the calls and connections he had made turned into business and the

> *
>
> **Business-to-business networking is all about building relationships.**
>
> *

service he provided was better than his competitor. He eventually became the top commercial cleaner in his city.

CHAPTER 7
Let your Marketing Budget guide your Marketing Strategy

Most of the franchise owners we interviewed consistently reviewed their marketing budgets. They paid close attention to what marketing tactics were working. The information that came from analyzing customer surveys and interactions led them to better understand their customer. This information provided valuable insight into specific ways to get your customer's attention and keep it. The analysis guided important financial decisions. Many franchisees calculated the lifetime value of a customer to help guide marketing decisions and dollar allocations. One of our massage franchisees realized that her ideal customer stayed with her for at least two years, and spent somewhere between $1500 and $2500 in services and product. Allocating $100 dollars in advertising per client paid off.

One franchisee we spoke to in the restaurant industry admitted when he first got into business he thought all he needed was a nice visible location and the customers would just come. It was a wake-up call when he sat at his beautiful new location and no customers showed up. That's when he realized he had to go out and find his customers. He learned that there wasn't just one way to acquire customers—there were many ways that included direct mail, ads in community newspapers and magazines, donating food to community events, and social media. He spent time and money on all of them.

Before investing in print ads, one food concept franchisee explained how he looked closely at what his competitors' ads looked like. He wanted to see what their "call to action" was and how he could stand out with his design. Another franchisee, who owns a specialty shoe store, did not rely solely on the franchisor's national campaign. He created his own local TV and radio spots. He knew his ideal customers were not aware his concept existed and because of this, he spent 70 percent of his general budget on advertising. Spending that kind of money was important; but even more important was paying close attention to what each campaign revealed. He had monthly meetings with key employees to go over the numbers and determine best approaches for the next month.

Another of our interviewees owned a tutoring business. He learned from his consistent study of advertising dollars that his business was cyclical. Once he understood when his busy and slow periods were he carefully allocated marketing dollars accordingly. He got more bang for his buck by getting involved in the community during slower times and increased his print ads during busy times.

Many of the top 20 percent producers increasingly have turned to social media campaigns and have allocated a certain budget for these campaigns. They used some of their monthly marketing budget to pay providers for regular e-mail campaigns, blog copy, and posts on Facebook, Twitter, Instagram, and other sites. Routinely looking at the analytics on each site gave them more insight into who their customer was, and where they would most notice their return on their marketing dollars. Successful franchisees don't cut their marketing budgets in good and bad times. They either keep them the same or add to them in bad times to steal market share from business owners who cut theirs.

 **ACTION ITEMS**

▶ **Google your company.** Google your competition. Where do you rank? Where does your competition rank?

▶ **Be a secret shopper with your competition.** Find out from a customer's perspective how their product/service ranks and compare it to yours. What do they do better? What do you do better?

▶ **How is your competition marketing their brand?** Compare their marketing with what you are doing.

▶ **Interact with Yelp.** Visit it regularly and respond to customer complaints.

▶ **What community fundraiser or organization could you get involved with?** Who can you partner with in the community to have your own fundraisers?

▶ **Build referral sources by building relationships, even if they do not at first lead to business.** When you are out in the community, be friendly, strike up conversations from a place of curiosity, and see where it may lead you.

▶ **Review your marketing budget monthly to determine what is and is not working.** Look for trends in your marketing strategies and don't rush to conclusions. Give those strategies some time to work.

SECTION TWO:
METRICS

CHAPTER 8
Mind Those Metrics

Before investing in a franchise business, many new franchisees obsess on how much gross and net profit they can expect in years one through five, when they can expect a return on investment (ROI), and what overhead expenses they will incur. Unfortunately, many new owners get so caught up with operations, marketing, sales, and management in their first year or two that they stop looking at their numbers on a consistent basis. They don't pay attention to what is coming in, and what is going out, month to month. Reviewing numbers takes a back seat to everything else. Many franchisees admit they don't like looking at numbers. Their eyes glaze over and they check out when looking at spreadsheets, as they would much rather be out selling or working on new marketing approaches.

Our top 20 percent producers use metrics regularly, not only for their marketing campaigns, but also for guidance with their business strategies. They pay close attention to their numbers. They make it a bi-weekly and/or monthly practice. Numbers serve as a guide to understanding buying trends, customer behaviors, business cycles and wasteful spending. Several of our top producers admitted that they did not pay attention to their numbers for the first few years as business owners. This oversight cost them in many ways. Once they started to pay attention to their business metrics they realized the areas where they could save a lot of money and where they could redirect income. Our successful franchisees used their numbers to compare prior months and years with current numbers. They found important pieces of information that helped them run more efficient businesses. They were better able to control costs and adjust spending on marketing tactics. They changed vendors when necessary and adjusted payroll to balance cash flow. Analyzing numbers helped guide important decisions. Our interviewees shared that paying attention to numbers gave them a sense of control and reduced anxiety. It also increased monthly and annual profits. A franchisee who owned a large senior-care franchise admitted she didn't even know what a P&L was when she started. She knew data and she knew the art of medicine, but she didn't know about profit and loss statements. However, once she learned how to read and use them, she routinely focused on profit and loss metrics and found that sharing some of the information with staff was a great motivational tool—for herself *and* her staff.

A small business-to-business franchisee shared that he had a constant eye looking at the bottom line so he always knew what next year should look like. He knew how many sales calls he would need to make to hit his profit goals. His philosophy is "If I am not doing something today, I will not get paid in twenty four months' time."

Another franchisee running a maid service put it pretty simply. She said, "Know your economics (your formula, what you charge based on what your market can afford and what you pay your employees)."

In another example a staffing franchisee shared how he used metrics as a way to hold his employees accountable. He kept a chart on the wall with key metrics that reflected daily and weekly activities such as the number of marketing calls, how many calls turned into interviews and how many placements were made. He told us that the moment a new employee is hired, he or she is made aware of what kind of numbers are needed to achieve the businesses goals and what activities are needed to achieve the numbers. His weekly sales meetings were action plans for making and meeting his business goals. He was not aware that any of the other franchisees in the system had developed this practice and was convinced it was what kept him in the top 20 percent performer range.

A last example was from a footwear franchise owner who spends more than half his revenue on a marketing budget. He disclosed how critical it was to look at numbers weekly so he and key players on his team could make detailed and important changes with their marketing strategy. He explained how he meets monthly with his media buyer to go over numbers and meets every two months with his entire team to focus specifically on numbers, projections, and action plans. He believes that had he not reviewed how much of his sales came from expensive TV and radio ads, he would have gone out of business. Some of the ads worked, while others didn't—paying consistent attention to sales generated from advertising kept clear what did and didn't work.

> *
>
> **It's just as important to obsess over metrics when running a business as it is when making the decision to buy a business.**
>
> *

A favored practice among some of the top producers was using metrics proactively to compare net and gross revenues and cash flows with other franchisees in their systems. This practice helped them see where they could improve. If other franchisees in their system were doing better, they want to know what they could do differently and adjust.

Our interviews revealed that franchise rock stars either stay on top of the numbers from the beginning, or learn the hard way to stay on top of them. They look at them, talk about them with employees, learn from them and adjust accordingly. For those that outsource their accounting tasks, they still stay on top of what the numbers show them about their business. It's just as important to obsess over metrics when running a business as it is when making the decision to buy a business.

 # ACTION ITEMS

▶ **Look at P&Ls bi-monthly.** Notice what expenses have gone up, and what have gone down. Look at your sales cycles. What is your best seller, and what is not? When do you sell the most and when the least? Make decisions about marketing, staffing, expenses, and purchases based on what the numbers tell you.

▶ **Ask other franchisees how they keep expenses down**, and what their best sellers are.

SECTION THREE:
RESOURCES

CHAPTER 9
Leverage Your Resources

"My business coach and I talked at the end of the year about goals for the next year. If there was something that was supposed to be accomplished in January, he'll call and ask if I got there, and I want to be able to say yes."

BOB WHITE, THE MAIDS FRANCHISEE

People who purchase a franchise have numerous reasons for doing so. Aside from having a tried and true system to follow, and no desire to reinvent the wheel, people buy a franchise because of the expertise and support that comes with it. They are purchasing something larger than just their own business. They are purchasing resources that they can tap into at any time to help them develop their business. They are purchasing the rights to be part of a business community and have access to all the other business owners in the system. They are part of a partnership where they are in business for themselves but not by themselves.

Unfortunately, many franchisees do not exercise those rights. They don't lean on their franchisor for help, and they don't integrate their business with the larger franchise community. Because we did not interview the bottom 80 percent producers, we are not sure why many of these franchisees don't reach out. What we do know from the top producers we interviewed was that they all trusted the franchisor and saw their franchise community as something akin to an advisory board. As one of our franchisees explained, "When you buy a franchise, it comes with a ready-made mastermind group. That's really the reason many people buy a franchise—so you don't have to reinvent the wheel. You also have the expertise of many owners running the same business as you. There are business owners who have been in your franchise anywhere from a month to thirty-five years or more, and many of them have been successful at executing the same business model you purchased. They are there to contribute to your success, and are some of your best resources." Unfortunately, many franchisees do not tap into the system of support as often as they could. A lack of trust may explain a part of this.

> ❋
>
> **When you buy a franchise, it comes with a ready-made mastermind group.**
>
> ❋

CHAPTER 10
Surrender to the System

"I had to resist my urge to change up the way they had suggested and just follow the model and the system. I broke even in two months."

SCOT BRADISH, **SNAP** FITNESS FRANCHISEE

According to Patrick Lencione in his book *The Five Dysfunctions of a Team*, the key to establishing trust is the ability to be vulnerable with others. Being vulnerable as a business owner can include admitting what you don't know and sharing with others what you are not good at doing. Your weaknesses can be related to your personality (do you readily trust others or are you wary of others) and to your skills and experiences (I don't know anything about marketing or I couldn't sell gloves to an Eskimo). When you join any group for the first time, you have to put yourself out there if you want to build relationships.

New franchisees have to be prepared to be vulnerable if they want to be in a partnership and become part of a community. They have to be willing to let their franchisor in on what they know and don't know, and what they do and don't do well. They have to be willing to surrender to the system and follow what they are being told to do regardless of what they think is best (after all, they are paying someone for their expertise). This, however, may be easier for people without prior business ownership experience than it is for people who have owned businesses in the past. It also may be easier for people who aren't suspicious of other people's motives from the get-go. Franchisees willing to surrender to the franchisor don't question the motives of the franchisor, and don't fixate on how much they pay franchisors in royalties and other fees.

A number of our top producers readily admitted that having business experience can be a detriment to a franchisee, especially when a franchisee thinks he or she knows better than the franchisor. They shared with us that it was easier to trust their own gut instincts at first than trust that the franchisor knows what to do and how best to implement the business. These producers learned early that they were putting their business in jeopardy when they didn't trust the franchisor and didn't follow the system. In order to reach that top tier, these franchisees made changes. They opened themselves up to their franchisors' guidance and input. A common theme for our franchisees who had to figure this out over time was expressed by one interviewee who said, "Our franchisor had a really good [business] plan, and I wanted a plan I could follow. When I followed the plan, I did well. When I decided my way was better, I wasn't nearly as successful with my ideas. I stick with the plan much more carefully now."

For our top producers who trusted the franchisors from the very beginning, the benefits were recognized early. They understood that following the system distinguished them from other franchisees. One owner explained that, "When I joined [the franchisor], I committed to do what the franchise system told me to do regardless of my opinion or gut reaction or what I thought I should do. There is a risk in going against my own opinion. It feels wrong and uncomfortable and unnatural. Say I have a problem with a customer and the franchisor tells me this is the way to handle it and I think otherwise. Regardless, I always follow what they say and I think that sets me apart from the other owners—my willingness to constantly learn and change the way I do things for the good of the overall operation. Most people aren't willing to change who they are or what they do." Our top producers followed the system as much as they could, and made changes when requested to do so because they understood that they were giving in to a system that was designed for their success.

> *
>
> **For our top producers who trusted the franchisors from the very beginning, the benefits were recognized early. They understood that following the system distinguished them from other franchisees.**
>
> *

CHAPTER 11
Partner with Your Franchisor

"My franchisor was always motivational and supportive. They were all superstars at running the system. They invested in me to get better. Always positive."

JOHN BOTSKO, BRIGHTSTAR CARE FRANCHISEE

ranchisees that trust their franchisors see them as partners, and they work together to build the franchise system. When we interviewed our top producers and asked them if they thought their relationships with their franchisors were more like a friend, partner, or policeman, the majority told us they felt that their franchisors were partners. The franchisor/franchisee relationship typically unravels when franchisees don't see the franchisors as partners and doubt their franchisors' intentions and goals. When the relationship is negative, and the franchisor is seen as an enemy, a franchisee's business often suffers. When the relationship is positive and the franchisee sees the franchisor as a business partner, positive things happen. This orientation around a positive partnership is reflected in our interviews.

"The place where most franchisees fall on their faces is in the nature of the relationship that they build with the franchisor. The franchisor is not a corporate monolith like many of the companies people have worked for prior to becoming franchisees. The franchisor is made up of individuals who are sitting by their phones ready to find out from you what they can do better to serve you and all of the other franchisees."

"People at corporate were great coaches and cheerleaders. If you have a tough time, they are right there. They believe in customer service as the cornerstone of their business and they treat us like customers. When their support staff coaches us, it really helps. They help us stay accountable to our goals and are very positive."

"I see our franchisor as a business partner. They are our friends, but without the difficulty of doing business with friends. They really are a partner. My success affects their success. If I am growing my business, they grow their business."

These comments make sense given that the overwhelming majority of franchise models are designed so that the franchisor makes money when their franchisees make money. Therefore, it behooves franchisors to help their franchisees. As one top producer said, "Because we affect one another, they [the franchisor's staff] do whatever they can to help me."

Top producers understand that the franchisor and the franchisees are all driven toward the same end goal. They see themselves tied to the future of the franchisor, and take responsibility for not only their success, but the franchisor's success as well. They "use the franchisor religiously, and [as a result] find the franchisor very beneficial." Bob White shared how he aligned his operational goals to the operational goals of the franchisor so that they shared the same one, five, and ten year strategic plans. He said, "it was imperative to my success to work on the same things they were doing."

Top producers whose goals are aligned with their franchisors' goals recognize what the franchisor brings to the partnership. On the way toward perfecting the system, franchisors have already made the mistakes and corrected missteps so franchisees don't have to. As one of our interviewees explained, "The franchisor has the benefit of watching what all the franchisees are doing, what is working and what is not, and then they share the information with all the other franchisees. This is a reason why I trust them to know what is best." Because the franchisor has access to what most of the franchisees in the system are doing, successful owners trusted that, over time, their franchisors would have integrated best practices into the system and made changes when necessary. Franchisees don't have to guess what does and doesn't work.

In addition to recognizing the value of a business model that is proven, our franchise rock stars recognized that they could not be successful without their franchisor's direction, guidance, and procedures. The consulting provided by the franchisors helped our interviewees develop goals and stay accountable for making sure the goals were met. Franchisors would listen to their franchisees whine, and talk them off the ledge. They also encouraged them to develop business and make sales calls. They were sounding boards for complaints and springboards for the testing of new ideas. Most importantly, the franchise owners focused on how the franchisor "could help them, rather than what they will do for them." They did not expect the franchisor to make sales calls and send them leads. Franchisors made sure franchisees understood what and how to do things and then helped them implement the ideas and plans.

For our respondents, franchise success required trust and mutual responsibility. They understood that their success led to the franchisors success. They called the franchisor

> *
>
> **They did not look to the franchisor to solve all their problems; they looked at the franchisor as a partner who knew what was best because they had *more experience.***
>
> *

when something wasn't working, and listened to their advice and implemented their systems, even if it meant going against what they thought was better. They did not look to the franchisor to solve all their problems; they looked at the franchisor as a partner who knew what was best because they had *more experience.*

CHAPTER 12
Partner with Other Franchisees

"I wished I would have relied on other franchisees in my system earlier in my development. I would have made a lot fewer mistakes."

SCOTT SURYAN, MAUI WOWI FRANCHISEE

"At annual conventions we learn so many new things. Many of the franchisees don't go. They say they can't afford it. We would talk to other successful franchisees at the conventions and then adopt the same practices. It was a great opportunity to talk to the most successful people in the system."

DAN AUSTAD, GOOD FEET FRANCHISEE

Our top producers see themselves in business with others rather than being in business by themselves. We heard from most of our interviewees that their businesses were part of a community that exists both inside and outside the walls of their business. Their community includes the folks who are part of the franchisor's corporate team, other franchisees in their system, and (as we will see in a later chapter) employees. They leveraged each of these resources to build and grow their businesses, and they believe this is what separates them from their less successful peers.

For franchisees that understand the value of being part of a larger system, it is easy to reach out to peers. While not all of our successful producers understood this at the outset, they all understood it over time. To reach out for help is not easy for many folks. As we commented on earlier, it requires an ability to be vulnerable and let people know you need help. For those who can be vulnerable and reach out to other franchisees, the rewards are great. As a Gotcha Covered franchisee expressed, "The reason I wanted to buy a franchise was to feel like I was part of a community. I was coming from corporate America and when I first started the business, I worked from home. Being by myself all day long was a big adjustment. If I was going to be successful, I needed to call another owner every day to have someone to talk with about business. If I had to do it alone or only with a couple of employees, it would have taken me a lot longer to be where I am. Your peers are people to bounce ideas off of and partner with to market and sell your services or products. The opportunity to collaborate with any number of peers is a perk. There is a lot you can learn from people who have been running your same business."

Finding out what your peers are doing to be successful is one of the easiest ways to improve your own chance of success. Our top performers saw that their success was tied to how much they contributed to and learned from other franchisees. They visited and called their peers, hosted their peers in their businesses, and attended conventions and regional meetings. By connecting with peers, franchisees can see things they are NOT doing. They can analyze, absorb, and apply what they learn. What the franchise owners often found when they spoke to or visited their successful peers was that their peers were simply following the system. They shared with us that less successful franchisees, who didn't leverage their peers, were making their biggest mistakes.

One owner who runs a sign business shared with us conversations he had with a peer. The peer continuously talked about his need to get out in front of customers face to face in addition to selling on the phone or through e-mail campaigns. This information reinforced what our top producer had heard from his corporate office, but the information didn't sink in until he heard it frequently from another franchisee. By getting out of his office and physically getting in front of decision makers, he understood what others had been trying to tell him: business comes down to building relationships with people. Getting in front of people that will buy from you is the first step. The sign business owner realized he was too dependent on cold calling, and changed his sales process as a result of these conversations.

Visiting other owners was a major theme for our top producers. An auto repair franchise owner shared with us that he regularly drove four hours to visit the owner of the second-highest-performing store in the country. The whole idea of having a franchise is to use the experiences of others to create a repository you can draw on to improve your own marketing, sales, and customer service. One successful owner explained to us that "if you take the time to visit the top two to four franchisees in your system, you will get one or two good ideas from each one as you see how they interact with customers and employees. If you implement any of the ideas, your business is sure to improve. You need to be able to talk to people." Top producers have a tight network of franchisees they can talk to at any time. For example, one person we spoke to calls three to four franchisees every week and talks about operations, marketing, and other issues. He runs ideas by them and sees what their thoughts are. He told us, "You have to be a people person to be a successful franchisee. You need to be able to talk to people." Their franchisee peers are friends, so they feel comfortable picking up the phone at any time. They are interested in learning about what does and does not work in their area or part of the country and are curious to see what others do. They share what is working or not, and

> *
>
> **If you take the time to visit the top two to four franchisees in your system, you will get one or two good ideas from each one as you see how they interact with customers and employees.**
>
> *

they are open to criticism and feedback. Then they use the feedback to benefit themselves and their business.

While being open to learning and being open to criticism is not easy for many folks, it is also not easy to reach out to folks you don't know or folks who you see doing very well. Rocky Gill summed this up for us in his interview. "I learned early on that I needed to make friends with top producers. I thought it would be hard because they wouldn't know who I was. I asked their permission to help me and over time, they have become my best friends. I figured if I could hang around them, I could be in the top 20 percent of the franchise. I had to overcome my hesitation that I was just one of the bunch of owners, so that I could talk to them. If you spend time with successful people, you will become a successful person."

Another easy way for franchisees to connect with one another is at annual or biannual conventions. While lower-performing franchisees might say they can't afford to go, our interviewees told us that you can't afford not to go. The winners in the system are at the conventions, so it makes it easy to learn from them. These meetings are also opportunities for franchisees to see recent developments in their industry, new marketing methods being rolled out by their franchisors, new products and services, new software, and new methods for delivering goods and services. One franchisee told us that after two years of owning her franchise, she finally made it to her first annual convention. Not only did she gain knowledge of new social media skills, she attended a breakout session on conflict resolution. What she learned and utilized from the session reduced her employee turnover. At these conventions, there are mastermind groups, sales trainings, business planning and strategy sessions, and plenty of opportunities to socialize with others that are part of your system. One franchisee told us that a couple months before the annual conventions he writes down what he wants to accomplish for the year and looks for help and answers there. The beauty of a franchise system is there are so many people out there who have done what you do. They have the credibility when they give you the right answer because they have walked in your shoes.

 **ACTION ITEMS**

▶ **Find out who the top performers are in your system.** Reach out to them to learn more. Mine them for information and implement the ideas they share.

▶ **Follow the system,** even when it feels counter-intuitive.

▶ **Go to franchise conventions.** Use them to build relationships and get new information and ideas. Have a system for implementing new ideas.

▶ **Ask your franchisor for help.** Use them as springboards for brainstorming new marketing approaches, decisions, and handling customer service issues that arise.

▶ **Hire an outside business mentor,** business coach, or join our business mastermind group to explore new ways to find and keep customers, increase sales, and improve your management/leadership skills.

SECTION FOUR:
LEADERSHIP

CHAPTER 13
Managing and Leading

"I think the greatest gift that we can give our team members is to develop their ability to be 100 percent responsible for their future. Reliable employees share the burden."

LINDA SKROMME, FAST SIGNS FRANCHISEE

A typical franchise business comes with a proven system, training, support, and a clearly prescribed set of procedures to follow. For most franchises, their training programs can be anywhere from one to five weeks, and typically cover the proprietary nuts and bolts to the business model: daily operations, sales, finance, marketing, software technology, and basic hiring practices. Often missing from franchisors' training programs is teaching what it takes to manage and lead employees. Based on our combined two decades of executive, entrepreneur, and frantrepreneur coaching, we have seen that some people have the skills to manage, some have the skills to lead and some have both. Many owners have neither. Some of our interviewees were natural leaders and/or had some experience with management and leadership roles before investing in a franchise. The majority, however, did not. They learned from their missteps and/or paid attention to what other successful leaders in their systems did. Our interviews revealed that management and leadership skills were key ingredients in the secret formula for franchisee success.

As we mentioned in the last chapter, top franchisees see employees as a valuable resource inside their business and take advantage of this resource. Employees of any business are brand ambassadors. They have the potential to represent your business well or represent it poorly. How you treat them goes a long way in determining how they represent your business and treat your customers. While it is true that employees have to understand the business model and know what is expected of them so they can perform their responsibilities, it is also true that they must have a desire to do the best job possible. We all know the difference between dealing with employees who love their jobs versus employees who hate their jobs. Every one of the franchisees we interviewed understood the value of having a good team and knew what it took to hire and develop a good team. Our top producers knew that after

> *
>
> **The commitment to train and empower employees trickled down to a rich customer service experience, which ultimately translated into more sales.**
>
> *

selecting the right people, one of their most important responsibilities was to become a full-time trainer. Putting the time into cultivating a good team took consistent commitment, and a process that involved ongoing accountability and follow up. The commitment to train and empower employees trickled down to a rich customer service experience, which ultimately translated into more sales.

CHAPTER 14
Know Who to Hire

Learning from hiring the wrong employees was a slow and costly process for many of our interviewees. Business owners typically hire folks from ads they place on job boards, websites like Craigslist and Indeed.com, or referrals from friends or family. Many owners start by hiring the cheapest labor they can find. Others hire with a focus on a particular set of skills or experiences. What our owners had come to see is that it often costs more money to deal with high turnover than it does to find the right people who are good fits for their businesses. Having clarity around what you are looking for in an employee for a specific job is the first step of the hiring process. Most of our respondents shared that what they first thought they needed from an employee was not what they actually needed. They learned that they really needed employees who were teachable, competent, competitive, service-oriented, motivated, and detail-oriented.

The most common employee characteristics that our successful franchisees looked for was "a head for service" and a positive attitude. As Rich Emory of Service Master Clean said, "If we can really care about customers' needs first, everything will take care of itself." In order to hire great people, Emory watched how employees served people whenever he was out in the community. He'd observe how they handled customers, their personality and their attitude. If he liked what he saw, he would hand people his card and say "if you ever need work, call me." We were surprised to learn in our interviews that industry experience was not nearly as important as was attitude, even in franchise businesses that required blue collar skills. Our top producers understood that they could train for skills and ability. They couldn't train for personality and attitude. Therefore, they look to hire upbeat personable people who are focused on getting the job done. They look for employees who are confident and open to learning what it takes to be successful. They want employees who are driven, ethical, self-motivated to perform, and enjoy the tasks/jobs that owners don't like doing. They looked for employees who are committed to customer service, committed to learning, committed to making the work environment fun, and committed to the vision of the business.

> *
>
> **Our top producers understood that they could train for skills and ability. They couldn't train for personality and attitude.**
>
> *

One example of changing the way employees were hired came from Jim Kabel of Case Handyman. He had high turnover when he first started out. It seemed like he was always looking for new help and it took up a lot of his time to interview and then train new hires. He began with the mindset he had to hire people with home repair expertise. His thinking was, "If they had the skill set, it would be easy to train them on company culture, values, and attitude." He came to realize it was the exact opposite. Just because they had a skill set didn't mean they would be great brand ambassadors. He admitted he felt foolish for being afraid to hire for performance skills rather than just vocational skills. Once he adjusted what he thought he needed, his business changed. He eventually hired employees he could count on, and who contributed to the well-being and growth of the business.

Another hiring practice shared by our interviewees was hiring folks who had different personalities or skill sets from the owner's. One of our franchisees, Dean Bingham of Mr. Transmission said, "An owner has to know his strengths and weaknesses." He believes it is important to hire people who "can take up the slack for your weaknesses." Franchisees shared that they hired people to do the things they didn't like to do or "played at what the owner worked at." They hired people who had expertise beyond their own. If owners weren't sales people, they hired sales people. If they didn't enjoy administration, they hired people who did. If owners were introverted, they hired extroverts, and if they were disorganized, they hired people who were organized. One retail franchise owner noticed how she enjoyed being on the floor and talking to customers. Her strengths were in building relationships. She disliked administrative tasks like bookkeeping, inventory management, and marketing. As things started to slip through the cracks, she took an honest look at what she didn't like to do and found people to do those jobs.

Another theme that was prevalent in our interviews was the need for

> *
>
> **Franchisees shared that they hired people to do the things they didn't like to do or "played at what the owner worked at."**
>
> *

employees to share the vision and values of the owners. Our franchisees recognized that the vision and values of their businesses created the culture of their businesses. Culture started at the top and then trickled down to all employees. Top franchisees wanted people who lived and breathed their vision, which often included being trustworthy, caring about people, being dedicated to customer service, and performing tasks at a high level. They shared their vision and values during the hiring process. One franchisee shares his company's vision, mission, and values in the initial interview and observes how candidates react. If they were excited about the mission and vision and asked questions, there was a good chance they'd make the second interview. Having an idea of where the company is going, prospective employees can see themselves as part of the big plan. Having prospective employees talk about their role in that plan is important in the hiring process.

Successful franchisees also make sure that peer interviews are part of the hiring process so that current employees not only have a say in new hires, they also can detect things that may go unnoticed by the owners. They understand that their employees have to share the owner's commitment to grow the business. By engaging employees in their culture, values, business and hiring processes, and metrics, they have employees who believe the business is theirs too.

When employees don't share their owners' vision and values, successful franchisees are quick to let them go. Dana Raley of Sports Clips said the best decision she ever made was to hire slow and fire fast. Taking the time to find the right hires, and getting rid of employees who were not the right fit as soon as possible is a strategy employed by our top producers. As one franchisee shared, "Warm bodies do not equate to a profitable business." Because every person in a business matters, "you need to be ruthless about moving on when people are not the right fit."

After too many mishaps trying to hire the right people for the right positions, one franchisee decided to take a different tact. He did the

> *
>
> **"Warm bodies do not equate to a profitable business."**
>
> *

job of an employee he would like to hire so he understood what the day-to-day aspects of the job entailed. He spent time working in a position to see what his employee would need to know and what he or she would need to do. It wasn't until he worked the job of his employee that he discovered that problem solving was a bigger part of the job description than was selling. He knew he had to find sales people that were problem solvers. The experience taught him to ask completely different questions in the interview process than the ones he had been asking. Rather than ask applicants more generally how they solve problems, he would give them real situations or problems he had dealt with and ask them how they would attempt to solve these issues. Those candidates that were comfortable with problem solving on the fly were the ones he would hire. Having the right people in the right positions doing the right kind of work solved his retention issues.

CHAPTER 15
Develop Your Employees

"Everybody has his or her role and you cannot be the master of everything. I knew in order to be effective I needed help in certain areas."

BEN KNIGHT, FAST SIGNS FRANCHISEE

S ome of the most popular goals for buying a franchise are: 1) to be your own boss, 2) to have flexibility over your schedule, and 3) to control your future. Many franchisees struggle with how to utilize their employees to help them achieve their goals. When franchisees find themselves working far more hours than they did when they worked for someone else, they often question whether becoming a business owner was worth it. Exhaustion and alienation from friends and family that comes from long days, seven days a week, can easily lead to burnout.

We found in our interviews that our top producers all had or developed an ability to "let go" and use the people resources that were available to them so that they could focus on growing their businesses rather than working in their businesses. While they might have begun as owners who did jobs they didn't like to do, or were not good at, or did every job themselves to insure it was done right, they learned that having too broad a job description was not a sustainable business model. Burnout and utter exhaustion forced them to look for other ways to operate their day-to-day business. Some of these franchisees admitted they had stress-related health issues that forced them to do things differently. Through trial and error and help from outside support such as their franchisors and business mentors or coaches, they found ways of implementing processes and systems to keep their businesses running more efficiently. Delegating duties to employees not only freed up their time as owners, it empowered their employees to make decisions and take more responsibility. Our interviewees learned to outsource what they couldn't do or didn't want to pay an employee to do.

When our franchisees gave themselves permission not to do everything in the business, they let others take on more responsibility. Our owners found growth to happen at a much faster rate when they delegated and followed up with employees. One example of learning how to delegate came from a senior care franchisee who admitted that despite the fact she had a good staff, she continued to wear all the hats in her business. When the pain of exhaustion and frustration finally impacted her life, she looked for some solutions. She looked at her weaknesses and accepted them. She decided to write down all the daily tasks she did and logged each one in a book for a week. After looking at all the hats she wore, she understood why she felt the way she did. She circled the tasks she enjoyed doing the most and checked the tasks she hated to do. This exercise allowed her to adjust her work tasks and created a better structure for delegating and reporting. She focused on doing the job she loved the most, interacting with clients and selling her services, while her staff focused on other tasks like marketing and management of staff. Delegating allowed her to make better decisions that affected the growth of the company.

Leadership is an Obligation to Grow Others

While delegating tasks was an important part of the way our successful franchisees ran their businesses, they also understood that they could not delegate without developing their employees. Employee development included initial training and ongoing training programs. It also included ongoing feedback to employees. They saw employee development as a way to increase loyalty and morale, and as an "opportunity to change the future of the country through influencing, developing, and provoking others to accomplish more than they currently have the capacity to accomplish."

Connie Worrel of Express Employment Professionals shared that she trained her employees the minute they walked in the door the first day and continued weekly trainings. Training alone was not enough. It was just as important to "inspect what I expect." She developed a regular system for giving encouraging feedback to her employees so they constantly knew how they were doing. She made it clear to all of her employees there was no such thing as a "dumb question" and encouraged employees to ask clarifying questions whenever necessary. Her open-door policy was a way for her to be accessible to her team so that she could nurture good decision making. This process allowed employees to learn from mistakes and motivated them to be as good as they could be at their jobs.

Rich Emory of Service Master Clean put it best when he said, "Our job is to make employees better people, not make better employees." He shared how he focuses training on how employees handle customers and serve others. "We try to instill our corporate objectives constantly. We develop, train, and educate managers and service partners continually in order to have the most knowledgeable staff in our industry. We want them to understand our corporate objectives and mission statement and understand that what they do affects themselves, our customers, our other employees, and the business. We all only succeed when we each succeed, and we instill in them during training that they are professionals serving professionals." Taking the time to develop employees in areas of communication skills, sales knowledge, and new marketing trends—using experts both inside and outside the business—helped

> ✳
>
> **"Our job is to make employees better people, not make better employees."**
>
> ✳

keep employees engaged and informed. One franchisee shared how he made room in his annual budget to take his employees off site twice a year for employee development days. He hired experts to lead them through communication exercises and sales techniques. An orientation around growing employees as people has a ripple effect. When employees feel taken care of in a rich learning environment, they feel integral to the success of the business. Happier employees impact other employees and customers.

The franchisees we interviewed understood their business was a team business and saw their primary job was to build a team and coach employees. Coaching began when the employees were hired. Our owners showed employees how to work by working side by side with them, and made sure their employees connected to the vision and values of the company by making it a point to include employees in important company decisions.

They coached their employees by continually providing goals for the future and helping their employees work toward those goals. One of our hair salon franchisees talked to each of his employees after their first ninety days and asked them how they'd like to improve. He shared that this was the best way to get employees to have buy-in to their own goals. There was always a date attached to goals, and he made a point of checking in with his employees every couple weeks to see where they were in their goal development. Rocky Gill, of Express Employment Professionals, shared, "If I don't lay out the goals and expectations and train employees to get there, shame on me. We train, serve customers, lay out a plan, and engage staff in the plan. We train our people the minute they walk in the door and continue to train every week."

Many of our interviewees also cross-trained their employees so their employees understood and could handle, most, if not all, jobs. One of our food service owners shared that cross-training his employees often saved him from having to come in on his days off. For our owners that had managers, they spent a great deal of their time developing their managers who would then be more effective leading employees. As Rich Emory of Service Master Clean shared, "If you put work and effort into creating a talented employee base, success happens." Our owners understood that the potential growth of the business was only as good as their team, and the success of their team depended on how much they were developed.

CHAPTER 16
Lead Through Transparency, Accountability, and Rewards

"I know each day how much gross revenue we need to bring in. I share this number with my staff. All employees get a payout incentive if they hit the number and exceed the number. When I was on vacation, the employees were concerned we would not make the numbers. So they came up with their own incentive and exceeded the numbers for the day. Everyone knows to look at the board."

BEN KNIGHT, FAST SIGNS FRANCHISEE

A s one top 20 percent performer put it, "The way to develop employees is through having them join you, not just by sharing your commitment, but also by owning your commitment." Our franchisees used accountability and transparency as a tactic for developing employees and nurturing commitment. They did so because they viewed their relationship with their employees as a partnership, much like the franchisor/franchisee partnership. By creating a team environment where everyone was working toward a bigger vision, the work environment became more collaborative, effective, and fun. Transparency included sharing their weaknesses with employees and sharing all aspects of the businesses with employees, including business plans and goals. Accountability meant sharing the expectations owners had for their employees and following up to insure tasks were done. Not only were employees held accountable, our franchise owners also made sure they were held accountable by their employees.

Our successful owners share what is happening in their businesses, and open themselves up to their employees' thoughts, ideas and suggestions regarding the direction, successes, and failures of the businesses. One franchisee shared how he and his employees shared their goals and objectives at monthly meetings. When he ran into challenges and obstacles with his goals, he shared them at these group meetings. This encouraged his employees to do the same and he felt that this transparency was instrumental in creating loyalty.

Our interviewees want their teams to push, question, challenge, and disagree with them. They want their employees to ask for clarity with respect to business plans, goals, and action plans. Employee input allows owners to adapt and make things better, and helps hold the owners accountable for achieving success. Our successful owners share decision-making, hiring, training, planning, and executing. They share business challenges and celebrate business successes with their employees.

Most of our franchisees look at financials weekly with their employees and set financial goals together. They share payroll information so employees understand what revenue is needed to make payroll, and what costs impact the bottom line. Employees who know a company's metrics know how many new customers translate to higher profits, and how keeping current customers loyal and happy adds to the bottom line. One auto repair franchisee devoted a half-day meeting explaining to the employees how much revenue the company needed to bring in to make payroll, how much revenue the company needed to make their first profit goal, second profit goal, and so on. As each profit goal was reached, employees shared in the profits through bonuses. He was very pleased as he explained the energy shift that occurred with his employees when he shared his numbers with them!

Transparent owners look at jobs or projects with their employees and ask what the company could do better. As a result, there is less uncertainty as to why decisions are made the way they are. Employees know why there are reductions, bonus cuts, and staff downsizing, as well as why bonuses are given and when new employees need to be hired. Everyone knows what part they play in the business plan and how they can affect the company's revenues and profit. Employees take responsibility because they buy into the business goals and plans, and have ownership over business outcomes. As a result of sharing information with employees, our owners found their employees' goals were often higher than what they themselves might have set, and there was greater trust between employees and owners. In these businesses, employee satisfaction was high.

> *
> **Transparent owners look at jobs or projects with their employees and ask what the company could do better.**
> *

According to our franchisees, transparency fosters a sense that the business is everyone's business and everyone is in it together. One of our residential cleaning franchisees told us that he had heard rumors that his maids were resentful that he rarely showed up in the office. After losing customers because his maids were not as reliable as he needed them to be, he spoke with a couple franchisees and told them about his issue. They suggested he share with his employees his role in reaching the company's sales quotas. He told his team how he spent his time following up with customers outside the office and showed the maids how his efforts increased the amount of cleaning services his clients bought. His maids were more reliable over time and he lost fewer customers. He saw that having transparency as a core value kept office politics and gossip to a minimum so that everyone was on the same team. By conveying core beliefs and values in how their business operates and how they treat people, owners create camaraderie, and nurture great teams. According to our franchisees, their employees are happy and have very few problems with other employees, owners, and customers.

Along with being transparent, our successful franchisees made sure that when they assign tasks, employees know the due dates for those tasks. Their employees understand their responsibilities and know they will be held accountable for executing them. They also have employees hold one another accountable, not just for job tasks, but also for upholding the companies' core values, culture, and expectations. By creating a culture of accountability, our interviewees nurtured in their employees a greater sense of pride and ownership for their individual jobs. Employees were more aware of the impact their performance made to the overall success of the businesses, and were more aware of the impact other employees had on the companies. It was very common for owners to have charts on display where employees enter key metrics (for instance, how many marketing calls, interviews, and placements are made, and whether calls completed were high, medium, or low quality).

One food service franchisee was sick and tired of managers not holding employees accountable, so she instigated a nightly report. At the end of the last shift, the manger on duty closed out the night with a sales report and job task report that was e-mailed to the entire team. Every person who worked in the business from the kitchen staff to the food runners, would get the nightly report. When the employees exceeded their goals, there were all kinds of accolades that made everyone feel part of a team! When they didn't make a goal the manager had to do some analysis and be accountable for what was missing from the day. When employees are held accountable and hold each other accountable, there is little negativity and second-guessing in the business. As Bill Holden of La Vida Massage shared, "Everyone is accountable to each other and if we don't do what we are supposed to do, we let each other down."

While transparency and accountability keep employees engaged, our interviews also revealed that successful owners keep their employees motivated through recognition and rewards. Our franchisees have contests with their employees and use those contests to engage staff in marketing and sales. Owners give positive feedback and rewards for metrics employees reach. They provide earnings bonuses, gift certificates, and timeshare stays. On the whole, our interviewees said they pay higher salaries than their competitors and offer employee benefits. They get involved in their employees' lives and let employees know they care about them personally. They encourage their employees to root each other on, so employees feel valued and appreciated. Employees who feel valued are happier, and happier employees create a positive work environment that impacts how customers are served.

As Jeff Boehmer of Aussie Pet Mobile shared, "The biggest thing to emphasize is getting the right people, and making sure you are motivating them so they enjoy working for you and are trying to be as successful as you are. They need to feel like a partner." Owners need to emphasize how important their employees are, and give them as much training and positive feedback as they can. They should solicit input from employees to improve the business, and teach them how the business runs. Employees need to enjoy what they are doing, feel good about working for the owners and feel like they are growing as individuals and employees. In other words, once owners get the right people on the bus, they have to train and develop them. They have to give employees some say in the direction of the businesses and increase their responsibilities, while letting them know they are valued. If employees are to be successful, they have to know what success looks like, be accountable for it, and be rewarded when they achieve it. As one franchisee told us, he was amazed at how far recognition for a job well-done went with his employees. His model was not set up for monetary bonuses, so monetary rewards were rare. That said, a simple acknowledgement of a great job done in private or in a team meeting put smiles on his employees faces and created a culture where employees were empowered and engaged.

> *
>
> **Employees who feel valued are happier, and happier employees create a positive work environment that impacts how customers are served.**
>
> *

 **ACTION ITEMS**

▶ **Profile who your perfect employee candidate is.**

▶ **Hire for attitude first and skill set second.**

▶ **Develop a quality interview protocol.**

▶ **Delegate, delegate and delegate.**

▶ **Follow up with your employees** and hold them accountable (Inspect what you expect).

▶ **Develop your employees** through continual training.

▶ **Be transparent with employees.**

▶ **Encourage employees** to regularly contribute to the growth and development of your business.

▶ **Reward employees** both publically and privately.

▶ **Care about and value your employees.** They are the life blood of your business.

SECTION FIVE:
MINDSET

CHAPTER 17
Mind Your Mindset

"Mindset – make sure you are getting into this business for the right reason. The money you make is a byproduct of the success of your business and your love for the business and the clients."

MIKE LEE, AIM MAIL CENTERS FRANCHISEE

I n this last section we explore the thoughts and attitudes our owners have about their business. We refer to this as the "inside game." While the last four sections of the book explored what owners did within the physical space of their business, this section explores what happens in their heads with respect to how thoughts, perceptions, and attitudes impact their businesses, relationships, and lives. In putting together this section, we sorted through the qualities and characteristics of our owners and found that the inside game was revealed in many ways as they talked about their successes and failures. All the owners we interviewed approached their businesses with an undeniable confidence and the attitude that failure was not an option. They wanted their businesses to be big, and spoke of "winning" when referencing their goals and objectives. They shared a healthy relationship to fear and obstacles and embraced challenging situations. They all knew why they were in business and were 100 percent committed to working hard to achieve their goals.

We're not claiming that these franchise owners didn't have their moments of uncertainty, with the occasional meltdown and/or frustration, because they did. But their ability to bounce back quicker from setbacks without allowing fear to completely take over and paralyze them is what sets these owners apart from their peers. When their businesses were doing

> *
>
> **But their ability to bounce back quicker from setbacks without allowing fear to completely take over and paralyze them is what sets these owners apart from their peers.**
>
> *

poorly or they were failing in their execution, they reflected on their situation and proactively pushed through it to find solutions.

In our interviews, we found a common belief that perseverance and determination are necessary traits for a business owner's success. For our interviewees, perseverance meant doing something despite difficulty or delays in achieving success. Determination was a quality that drove them to continue to try to achieve things that are difficult. While these are both important traits, perseverance and determination without purposefulness generates less effort. Purposefulness is the rocket fuel that drives one to persevere and nurtures determination.

CHAPTER 18
Practice Your Purposefulness

"It's a belief you are in the right spot at the right time."

SHANE ORTELL, GOTCHA COVERED FRANCHISEE

Purposefulness as defined by many of our top producers is the desire to live life on your own terms. It means you are in business to make your mark in the world. You have a say in how you feel, and what you get to do. Purposefulness reflected what our owners care about. We discovered that being purposeful means asking yourself if you are clear on *why* you are owning a franchise/business in the first place. For our interviewees, it was never about replacing a job or salary with a business. It was for something more important, like leaving a legacy for their family, or building a future they had more control over. Purposefulness is why you want to make your mark on the world and how you intend to use your business to make that mark. Purposefulness means you are not willing to relax and let go until you achieve what you want to achieve. It entails determination and a refusal to accept failure. It is a quest that requires an owner to examine who he or she is, and whether or not he or she has what it takes to realize his or her dreams.

Successful franchisees must have the desire to live life on their own terms, and their reason for doing so is their purpose. It is about taking ownership of your life. For some people, their purpose is around providing excellent customer service. For other people, it is about supporting their community. For still others, it is about creating a legacy. Finding your purpose and acting on it really

> ✳
>
> **Purposefulness reflected what our owners care about. We discovered that being purposeful means asking yourself if you are clear on *why* you are owning a franchise/ business in the first place.**
>
> ✳

takes courage. Successful business owners do not let things stand in their way, and work hard to overcome obstacles and setbacks, because they have purpose.

One of our top performers, Anil Nanda, owned a franchise designed to help business owners reduce expenses. He was inspired to leave the corporate world to do something he called "playing the game of knowing myself." He believes entrepreneurs have the opportunity to continually improve and grow themselves in ways employees don't. He was sick and tired of watching himself and his coworkers live on the hamster wheel, just going through the motions in a corporate job with absolutely no purpose. He noticed that many of his coworkers and colleagues freely blamed others for their unhappiness, misfortunes, or mistakes. To Nanda, this was a clear symptom of not taking responsibility for one's own purpose in life. His desire to work for himself was to improve various aspects of his life. He loves that he can make a difference to a business's bottom line, but more importantly, he loves that he can be a role model for other business owners. His purpose is to make other business owners more successful by helping them tap into the mindset of a successful business owner. As he shared with us, "I like helping businesses find money, it's very rewarding. If I don't make sales calls, I deserve to starve. But, what is most important to me is to make my business work for my life, and what works for my life is helping others. By tapping into my purpose, I take full responsibility for my business rather than assign responsibility for my business to others."

Once Nanda made the decision to live life from a place of purpose, everything became easier. Purpose showed up not only in his profit margins, it served as a compass for building his future. His stress levels were down, and his relationships were better. "Taking full responsibility for my business rather than assigning responsibility for my business to others is the definition of purposefulness." According to Nanda, having a purpose was easily said, but not as easily done. "Just simply saying you have purpose is not the same as living from purpose. Purposefulness takes courage and discipline."

Nanda was convinced that the lack of purposefulness and the lack of "WHY" (knowing why you are in business) separates high performers from mediocre and low performers. He noticed that mediocre and low performers were more apt to complain and blame others when things did not work out for them. Having a purpose kept him out of the "blame game." He shared that "so many of the franchisees I have met over the years complain that the franchisor does not help them be profitable. I have learned that taking full responsibility and acting as if there were no franchisor to rescue me has been a great asset to my success. My purpose is to make my business profitable by helping others make their business profitable, and it is 100 percent my responsibility to make this happen." Nanda was adamant. He said, "I don't wait for anyone from the franchise to help me. I go after the help I need. Having a purpose drives me forward and if the franchisor helps me, great. If they don't, it is because I didn't reach out and am taking it on myself to create my own success."

He shared that when he asks franchisees to tell him about what problems they are having or what they feel is holding them back, many respond with things like, "My customers are nothing but a headache," or "My employees are bad or can't be trusted." His response is that they need to think of *themselves* as the problem and ask how their doing something differently might provide them with solutions. He explains to them that each owner sets the tone and example in their business. So if they can't trust employees or have terrible customers, it's because they have not set the tone and expectations for their people and the business, and ultimately, they have allowed these problems to happen. Business problems almost always lead back to the owner or person in charge of the business. Whatever owners are complaining about is most often a reflection of what is lacking with the owner. What Nanda was so eloquently able to convey was that when you lead from a place of purpose, you are more

> *
>
> **Business problems almost always lead back to the owner or person in charge of the business. Whatever owners are complaining about is most often a reflection of what is lacking with the owner.**
>
> *

apt to take 100 percent responsibility for your business because the business represents so much more than what you see on the surface. As coaches, we have seen that business owners frequently can't articulate why they are in business. When business owners can take the time to create a mission and vision statement that is true to who they are, they begin to find their purpose.

CHAPTER 19
Free Yourself from Fear

"You have to take each obstacle without fear. If you approach it from a non-fear perspective, just more matter-of-fact, you can solve the challenge."

LINDA SCHROMME, FAST SIGNS FRANCHISEE

"Don't let barriers stop us. If we have an obstacle we figure out how to overcome it. We find solutions. We are going to be successful—we are just that type of people. We set a lot of goals and work toward them."

DAN AUSTAD, GOOD FEET FRANCHISEE

Besides having a clear purpose around their businesses, our top 20 percent owners all shared that they had a healthy relationship to fear, obstacles, mistakes, and set-backs. Challenges and unforeseen circumstances are a part of business life. How an owner responds greatly determines their ability to be successful. Fear and obstacles either paralyze owners or motivate them. Mistakes and set-backs either derail owners or are seen as seeds for opportunity and growth. Successful owners know how to manage their fears and see obstacles and challenges as opportunities to grow. Rather than shutting down when things don't go well, they pick themselves up off the floor, kick off the dust and move forward. As one of our respondents shared, "If you crumble in front of obstacles, you'll fail."

> ✳
>
> **Successful owners know how to manage their fears and see obstacles and challenges as opportunities to grow.**
>
> ✳

Fear Requires a Change of Focus

Our interviewees all agreed that taking action changes their focus from what makes them afraid to what they can do to move forward. They ask themselves what they can do to remove their anxieties or fears and jump on those activities as quickly as they can. Rather than worry about losing customers, they focus on what would please customers and enhance their customers' experiences. Rather than worry about declining revenues, they focus on increasing sales activities. Rather than brooding alone about their anxieties or fears, they call their franchisors or other franchisees, or talk to outside coaches and/or mentors.

Many admitted in the first year of business they would freak out when there was a slow month. With no business history to rely on, they lost a lot of sleep and many were paralyzed with negative "what if" thoughts. Once they understood that business has cycles, they used the slower months to prepare for maximizing the busier months. Fear was indeed a paralyzer if they let it be. That said, if they were self-aware enough to notice it, they would acknowledge it, see it as an opportunity, and then move past it. Fear did not control them; they were able to control fear.

Some of them said that when they noticed fear, they were in growth mode. Fear was an impetus for growth. If there is no fear, there is complacency, and complacency means no growth. Doing nothing was extremely damaging, not only to these owners' businesses but also to their health. Several owners shared stories of how their health was affected by the immobilizing nature of fear when business was bad. One owner candidly shared about a time when fear nearly paralyzed him. His wife, who he described as a calm understanding woman, raised her voice when she saw him crying in his recliner. She told me "to get in the shower, quit crying and go make sales calls." It was great advice. He got up, got dressed and made sales calls. He said from that day forward he never wallowed again. Instead he remembered his dream (the "why" he got into business) and every situation where fear began to creep in, he used as a learning opportunity. These owners learned that being proactive was a great remedy and a great motivator. As one owner shared, "When I notice myself worrying about a decision, I know it's time to make one."

CHAPTER 20
Dealing with Failure and Mistakes

"I have made mistakes, and I am not afraid to make them. I will do something and if it doesn't work, I will fix it. I have figured out that a mistake is really an opportunity to learn. I embrace my mistakes. I love my obstacles—they are my indicators that what I am up to is bigger than me, and that gets me excited."

MIKE MACK, SERVICE MASTER CLEAN FRANCHISEE

Besides being proactive in managing fears, anxieties, and obstacles, our top producers see mistakes and failures as learning opportunities. Our owners acknowledge their mistakes and don't beat themselves up. Instead, they ask themselves what they will do differently the next time. They make changes because they see mistakes as fertile ground for growth and opportunity. As Cheri McEssy of Brightstar Care told us, "You don't wallow—you figure it out. Move on and be proactive." Our successful owners don't dwell on failure. Instead of focusing on what they are doing wrong, they focus on what they are doing right and/or how to do things better. They focus on their strengths and how to make the business stronger.

One franchisee told us he would actually walk himself through a series of questions when challenges came up. An example he gave was after dealing with a great deal of employee turnover, he finally asked himself, "What is the lesson here? What am I not seeing here, where can I make adjustments?" It took some introspection and when he dove deeper into his questions, he realized the issue was indeed fixable. He came up with a tighter training system, and used a follow up system that included accountability and acknowledgement of job responsibilities. His employees felt better connected to the business. Turnover went down, and he discovered that he really enjoyed developing his employees. In most of our interviews, respondents used their mistakes, both big and small, to make their businesses better. Many acknowledged that without painful mistakes their businesses would not have been successful.

> *
> **Our owners acknowledge their mistakes and don't beat themselves up. Instead, they ask themselves what they will do differently the next time.**
> *

CHAPTER 21
Playing a Bigger Game

Another aspect of successful franchise owners' mindsets has to do with their vision for their businesses. Our top producers set out with a desire to build big businesses. We call that desire "playing a bigger game." Playing a bigger game requires a Game Plan. It has rules associated with it, and incorporates a strong desire to win. Mike Mack, a Service Master Clean franchisee characterized this mindset when he said, "I love to win and I love the game of business. I'm not in it just for the money. I set out to build a business. I went into it with the idea that owning a business is not a job. I played the job game before and I lost. I was dead set on *not* playing that game. So I made a new target— creating a business that I love. I determined that it was unacceptable for me to not love every part of it. This was a totally new game. In order to achieve a business that I love, I created rules where the running of the business was as important as the score at the end of the game. One new rule was that it was not acceptable for me to do everything myself, so that I don't burn out. The rules called for me to surround myself with good people that compliment my skill set."

In other words, our interviewees did not buy a franchise to replace a job or salary, or be some "Chuck in a Truck" whose income is dependent solely on their effort. They got into business because they were passionate about wanting something substantial, and wanting to have a lasting impact. They welcomed the opportunity for growth from both a personal as well as professional standpoint. To grow something substantial, their game plan required time to work on their business and time to develop strategies for winning.

Most of our owners had plans for their businesses, and updated those plans regularly. They spent time working "on" their businesses rather than working "in" their businesses. They didn't "hide behind their operations," but rather led from the front. Our interviewees planned early on to grow their businesses to a significant size. For some it meant penetrating their market and for others it meant adding more territory or more locations. They took time in their week to plan, strategize, adjust, and reflect. They had lofty financial goals and personal goals, and worked toward achieving them. One of our maid service franchisees had goals to have a five-year payback on investment, be the largest franchisee in his system, and be out of running the day-to-day business after three years. Playing a bigger game, he said, was paramount to his success.

> *
>
> **Most of our owners had plans for their businesses, and updated those plans regularly. They spent time working "on" their businesses rather than working "in" their businesses. They didn't "hide behind their operations," but rather led from the front.**
>
> *

To achieve their goals, the franchisees set up rules. One rule was that they would not shy away from hard work. Everyone we spoke to acknowledged that what set them apart from their less successful franchisees was the amount they worked and how involved they were in the business. As one of our franchisees said, "It takes a bazillion hours a week to work your business and get it off the ground. If you are worried about the time involved to get your business up and running and successful, you shouldn't start a business. If you don't have the burning desire to work hard, don't even try it. If you are going to do it, be 150 percent in." While it is true that an owner can over time relinquish many responsibilities to employees (and many of our top 20 percent producers were at a point in their business when they could), it is crucial to understand that doing so early on in the life of a business is a recipe for disaster. As we have seen in our work with franchisors and franchisees over our combined twenty years, franchisees who are passive owners from the start rarely achieve the kind of success seen by owners who have worked on the business full time from the beginning.

Another rule our owners followed was that they would not do all the work. Playing a bigger game meant not trying to do everything themselves. They hired others who played at what they worked at, and outsourced tasks whenever they could. They set aside time with their franchisors or business coaches to strategize and implement their plans while their employees were responsible for day-to-day tasks.

A last rule we found our owners playing by was that owners had to enjoy what they did and be passionate about their businesses. As one of our retail franchisees shared, "You've got to love what you are doing. If you don't, you add negative emotions and get negative results. Passion leads to new ideas and those ideas let you stay fresh in your customers' eyes." Passion also helps you figure out ways to solve problems and get things done. Passion comes from having a purpose, and with passion comes focus and energy. Passionate owners eat, sleep, and breathe their business. They run their businesses because they want to, not because they have to. Passion translates to success.

Lastly, all our franchisees were oriented around winning and had lofty expectations for themselves and their businesses. John Botsko, a Brightstar Care owner, told us that when he started his business, he wanted to play the same game the founders of his franchise had

> *
>
> **Playing a bigger game meant not trying to do everything themselves. They hired others who played at what they worked at, and outsourced tasks whenever they could.**
>
> *

played. They were superstars in the industry and he was not going to stop until he replicated the same success. He was so impressed with the founders' passion and tenacity that he wanted to duplicate it. That was his game, and that is where his game plan came from.

Shane Ortel, a Gotcha Covered franchisee had the lofty goal of becoming number one in his franchise system. He hit $1 million in revenue by his third year. He was inspired to come up with his game plan when he observed other franchisees in his area and took note of what they were and were not doing. He went about doing things better and more strategically and developed a game plan that he continually adjusted.

In wanting to be top producers, our interviewees created and adjusted their business plans as necessary, organized their businesses so they could work *on* rather than *in* their businesses, and managed failures and setbacks by refocusing their energies and learning from their mistakes. They knew where they wanted to go and were focused on getting there. They had purpose and passion and created operating rules that drove them toward success. Determination, perseverance, fearlessness, and a burning desire to be at the top differentiated them from their less successful peers. What they brought to their businesses from within their minds made a considerable difference in what happened when they walked through the doors of their businesses.

ACTION ITEMS

▶ Define your purpose for having a business. Ask yourself *why* you are in business.

▶ Become aware of when *fear* is guiding your actions and decisions and take action.

▶ List the mistakes you have made in the last five years and ask what you have learned from them.

▶ Stop looking through a small lens at the potential of your business. Find the passion and what drives you to play a bigger game.

AND IN CLOSING

CHAPTER 22
Conclusion

The franchisees we interviewed subscribed to similar business philosophies. When it came to marketing strategies, they simultaneously used several different vehicles to reach their ideal clients and believed that consistently measuring the success of each vehicle was crucial to their marketing success. Their marketing plan was a community plan and they listened to what their numbers had to say about their business. Collectively, they defined management as the responsibility to develop great employees. They demonstrated this by their conscious effort to lead by example. Accountability and transparency were methods they shared to create harmony, discipline, and a sense of ownership with their employees. They surrendered to the franchise systems, and trusted that the franchisors had developed systems worthy of following. When they did stray, it had more to do with their understanding of their local markets and were encouraged by their franchisors for taking initiative. They bought into the idea that they invested in a franchise business to be in business for themselves and not by themselves. This meant they were active in their franchise systems and leveraged other owners and the franchisors' staff to grow their businesses and themselves.

Whether you are considering investing in a franchise, or are currently a franchisee, becoming a top 20 percent producer may not be as difficult as you might have thought. The concepts, thoughts, and ideas we gathered from these top 20 percent are the day-to-day practices needed to be in the top 20 percent in almost any franchise system. Fortunately, implementing the recipe is not particularly complicated. What we do outside of our business and how we think about our business matters. Hiding behind daily operations is not recommended, while stepping out from your operations is. Putting in place systems and processes around training, management, marketing, and finance, and being visible to your community, your clients and your employees matters. Getting buy-in from employees and ensuring that they and their owners hold one another accountable is part of the success recipe.

Successful frantrepreneurs get involved with their franchise systems, get involved with other franchisees, *and* get involved in their local communities. Leadership happens inside and outside the business. Successful franchisees utilize the entire franchise system to learn, to problem solve, and to grow. They are not running the businesses on their own but are in partnership with their franchisor, other franchisees, and their employees. Each one of the frantrepreneurs we interviewed had a sense of confidence about their abilities. They viewed challenges as opportunities, thrived on solving problems, and had aspirations that matched their sense of purpose. Their attitudes matched their aptitudes, and their focus on being top performers led to their success.

Reading a P&L monthly and using the information to tweak operations is a decision owners make. Having weekly and monthly management meetings that include accountability is a decision owners make. Tapping into franchise resources and approaching business with a positive attitude is a decision owners make. These decisions to act are what create good business habits, and come from practice, time, effort, and a commitment to implement them. Successful frantrepreneurs continuously strive to improve by acting on their values and beliefs, and leveraging the resources their franchise system provides. While it might be difficult to change your mindset and implement all the key ingredients we have shared, we do believe that the first step requires one change in one area, and we encourage our readers to take that first step. Doing more in one area of The Franchisee Formula is a multiplier for increased business success.

About the Authors

Dr. Marc Camras

Dr. Marc Camras brings fifteen years of organizational and human development experience into his executive and entrepreneurial coaching company. He founded MVision Consulting to support and challenge entrepreneurs, wannabe entrepreneurs, executives, and leadership teams from Fortune 500 and 1000 companies to accelerate their potential and achieve breakthrough growth. Passionate about provoking change, fostering leadership, and increasing business success, Dr. Camras uses one-on-one and group coaching, facilitation, and team building exercises to create a powerful culture of development, innovation, and change within small and large companies and organizations.

His clients are domestic and international leaders from large companies, government organizations, professional services, and family businesses. He has raised the profile of leaders from companies such as Dr Pepper Snapple Group, Epson, Foster's Wine Estates, Google, Gilead Sciences, Pharmavite, Roche, Ernst & Young, Wells Fargo, Charlotte Russe, Thermadyne, Honda, Booz Allen Hamilton, and De Lage Landen by provoking difficult conversations, enhancing confidence, and envisioning greater success. Additionally, he works with small business owners, non-profits, educational institutions, nongovernmental organizations, medical practitioners, and prospective entrepreneurs interested in owning their own businesses both domestically and abroad. In the past ten years, Dr. Camras has helped close to a 100 new "frantrapreneurs" launch their franchise businesses.

Secrets of Franchise Success is the culmination of his efforts to bring leadership and executive coaching into the world of franchising. After spending the past decade working with current and potential business owners to identify "great fit" businesses, and making sure that business owners have everything in place to ensure business success, Dr. Camras saw the need to help franchise companies better develop their business owners by providing management, leadership, and business coaching beyond the initial training franchisors provide. Identifying the characteristics of successful franchisees and learning about their best practices, Dr. Camras is committed to bringing simple, practical, and useful techniques to the large group of franchisees who have not achieved the success they envisioned when they started their business.

Dr. Camras received his training as an executive coach with the Center for Creative Leadership and is a board certified coach with the Center for Credentialing and Education. In addition, he is an affiliate broker/consultant with FranServe. He has a Bachelor of Arts in Psychology from UC Berkeley, a Masters in Human Development from Harvard, and a PhD in Communication from UC San Diego. Prior to his business career, he taught classes in communication, education, human development, and leadership. *Secrets of Franchise Success* is his first book.

Melissa Woods

In a career that spans over twenty-five years, Melissa Woods has been coaching entrepreneurs, facilitating the launch of new businesses, and discovering new market opportunities for existing businesses. Her supportive, knowledgeable, direct, and action-oriented style is what makes her uber-successful in helping entrepreneurs "get out of their own way" and become profitable and successful business leaders. She focuses on defining qualities that distinguish ordinary businesses from extraordinary businesses in marketing, sales, business development, and customer service. Woods regularly facilitates mastermind groups for CEOs, business owners, and executives.

Woods career started in the late eighties when she founded JW Tumbles, a children's gym, which grew into a successful franchise company, with over forty locations worldwide. As founder and CEO of JW Tumbles, Woods developed and facilitated franchisee-training programs, sales processes, and ongoing support systems, including comprehensive operating manuals. After selling her company, Woods joined OneCoach, an international small business coaching company. As director of coaching, she developed new programs, recruited, trained, and managed coaching staff while creating a streamlined format customized for small businesses

As a successful "in the trenches business owner," Woods understands what it takes to grow a business smartly and effectively and is passionate about helping business owners find simple solutions to everyday challenges while avoiding stress and burnout.

Her understanding of what it takes to be a successful business owner, a successful franchisee, and a successful franchisor comes from years of trial and error, working smart and selecting the right mentors to guide her. *Secrets to Franchise Success* is the culmination of her twenty plus years of business development and she is enthusiastic about sharing her wisdom.

An outdoor enthusiast Woods enjoys her free time with her friends and three daughters hiking, biking, and practicing yoga.

☐ YES, I am ready to be a top performing franchisee and take the first step.

The book gave me great suggestions for sustaining success. I would like support on developing strategies that work best for me and my business. Most importantly I would like help with simple steps needed to execute and a consistent support system for staying accountable.

Please have a Franchise Prosperity Institute representative contact me by telephone. I would like to know more about the Franchise Prosperity Institute Accelerator Program, as well as the Franchise Prosperity Institute Roundtable groups.

Name: _____

Company Name: _____

Phone Number: _____

Email Address: _____

Number of employees: _____

Years in business: _____

Three Easy Ways to Contact Us:
- Visit our website at www.secretstofranchisesuccess.com
- Email/Scan the complete form to
  Melissa@secretsoffranchisesuccess.com
- Call us at 866-960-9196

Made in the USA
Lexington, KY
05 November 2019